Clothing

Contents

What do they wear?

When fabric or cloth is made, a lot of thought goes into what it is to be used for. People who make clothes decide what **fibres** to use to make the fabric best suited for its job. Should it be thick, thin, warm or cool? Should it be waterproof or not? Should it be stretchy?

- Stretchy leggings that are easy to move about in
- Leotard that doesn't get in the way when dancing
- Sweat-shirt to help keep warm
- Comfortable shoes
- Ankle warmers for warmth and protection

- Tough denim jeans that don't tear easily
- Warm jumper that washes well
- Hard hat to protect head
- Strong shoes that won't be spoilt by mud

- White overall to protect clothes from flour and spills

- Hat to stop hairs falling into dough

- Thick oven gloves to protect hands from heat

- Padded jodhpurs that stretch and are warm and comfortable

- Warm jacket

- Gloves to keep hands warm and protect them from reins

- Hat to protect head in case of a fall

- Boots to keep feet dry when walking in muddy places

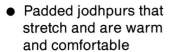

Draw two people who work in your school. What sort of clothes are they wearing? Are they wearing any special clothes for their job?

Fibres

A single strand of something is called a fibre. Fibres come from many different things. One of your own hairs is a fibre. Animals' fur or hair is made up of fibres. Plants have fibres in them. Artificial fibres can even be made from coal or oil. Fibres can be thick or thin. Can you think of any other fibres?

Spider thread is so light that a single thread stretched around the world would weigh less than three hens' eggs.

In Papua New Guinea, however, the fibres from some spiders' webs are strong enough to be used for fishing lines. These fibres come from spiders' webs which measure up to two metres across!

Plant fibres

Sisal factory in Kenya

Many fibres that we use to make fabrics come from plants. Some are hard, stiff and very strong. Sisal is very strong. It is used to make rope and twine. It can be woven into mats. Rafia is another plant fibre. It can be made into baskets and hats.

Cotton is a soft fibre. It comes from the **boll** or seed pod of the cotton plant. The fibres are short but they twist easily so they are easy to spin into threads. Cotton is also easy to weave into fabric and to dye different colours. Cotton is light and strong and it absorbs moisture. It is good for making summer clothes, sheets and towels.

Silk

Silk comes from the **cocoons** of silkworms. The cocoons are dropped into boiling water. The water loosens a cocoon's binding of long silk fibres. The silk is then spun into threads and woven into silk fabric.

The thread from a silkworm cocoon can be 800 metres long. That's so long that it would take you nearly ten minutes to walk from end to end!

Wool

Llamas

Wool is a fibre too. It comes from a number of different animals including sheep, goats, llamas, vicunas and alpacas. Wool grows on the skin of these animals. These animals are shorn regularly and the fibres from their **fleeces** are spun into woollen thread. After an animal has been shorn, a new fleece grows. It is rather like having a haircut!

Wool can be spun into thread which is woven into fabric to make clothes like suits, skirts and dresses. Woollen thread easily traps air between its fibres which helps keep us warm. This makes it good for blankets and winter clothes.

People who make clothes like to use wool because it is strong and hard-wearing and because it is warm, soft, stretchy and easy to dye. It is also comfortable to wear.

Threads

Fibres are not usually strong enough, long enough or thick enough to use on their own. They need to be twisted or spun together to make a **thread**. A thread is stronger than a single fibre. Here is someone who spins woollen fibres into thread:

> I still spin wool the way my grandmother used to. It takes a long time but I enjoy the work.

> First of all, I take a lump of wool from a sheep's fleece. The fleece has been washed to get all the dirt out. Then I comb or **card** the fleece to make the wool fibres lie in the same direction.

> Then I take the combed wool fibres off the card and start to spin them on the spinning-wheel. The fibres twist together and make a long woollen thread.

I sell the woollen thread that I spin to a woman who dyes it and then knits it into beautiful clothes.

Look at a piece of wool thread carefully. Can you see the fibres? Try unpicking the fibres. Can you see how they are twisted together? Look at some other threads like cotton and string. Are they made of twisted fibres too? What do these threads look like under a magnifying glass?

A spinning-wheel is one way of making fibres into strong threads. But spinning-wheels are slow and are not used in factories. There are many fast factory machines which spin fibres into threads.

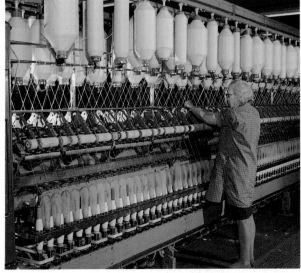

Cotton spinning mill

Knitting

Before threads can be made into clothes, carpets, curtains, sheets, tablecloths or anything else, they must be made into a piece of fabric or cloth.

There are a number of ways of turning thread into fabric. One way is to knit it. Knitted fabrics are usually quite stretchy.

2 Then the thread is pulled through the loops to make the next row.

1 Only one thread is used in knitting. A row of loops of thread is made with a pair of knitting needles.

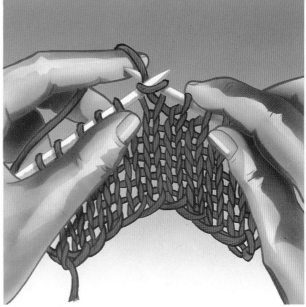

3 This is repeated many times until, eventually, a flat piece of knitted fabric is made.

4 Interesting patterns can be made by using different coloured wools or by changing the type of stitch. The stitches can be knitted into different patterns such as cables or lace.

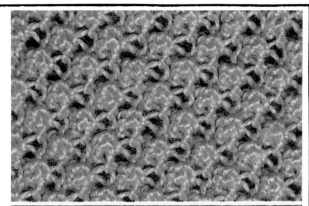

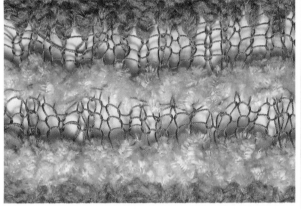

Most knitted fabrics are made in factories on knitting machines. They work very quickly and can be used to knit socks, tights and vests as well as jumpers. Some people have small knitting machines at home.

What clothes are you wearing today that are made out of knitted fabrics? Look through a magnifying glass at some knitted fabric. Can you see the loops?

Home knitting machine

9

An interview with Patricia Roberts

Patricia Roberts is a designer. She designs knitted garments (clothes). People buy the garments in fashion shops. She also designs knitting patterns, for people to knit clothes themselves. We asked Patricia Roberts about her work.

When you design a garment, what do you do?

First, I think about the kind of garment I want to make. I decide what **yarn** (thread) and stitches I want to use. Then I draw a picture to show what everything will be like. After that, I make a knitting plan. It's a kind of code. Knitters understand it. It tells them how to knit the garment, stitch by stitch. Sometimes I make a plan that doesn't work. Then I have to change the design.

When the plan is ready, what do you do?

I knit parts of it myself, to test it. Then I send it to our knitters. They knit the garments for me.

Who are your knitters?

Most of them are people who have another job as well. Knitting is their hobby. I use them because they're expert knitters. They knit garments for me in their spare time.

Do you send them the yarn as well?

Yes. All our yarn is special. People spin it and dye it exactly the way I want. We use three main kinds of yarn: wool, cotton and silk. We use natural fibres only. We never use artificial fibres.

Why not?

Artificial fibres are fine for machines to spin and weave. They make cheap, hard-wearing clothes. But I prefer natural fibres. I think that they look better, and feel better. They are more comfortable to wear. Also, each kind is different. Each gives me ideas for garments.

How are they different?

I think about the thickness of the yarn. I think about how strong it is. When it's knitted, how will it stretch? I think about how the fibre looks. Silk looks quite different from wool, for example. There are different kinds of wool. Angora wool comes from a special breed of long-haired rabbit. It looks quite different from sheep's wool.

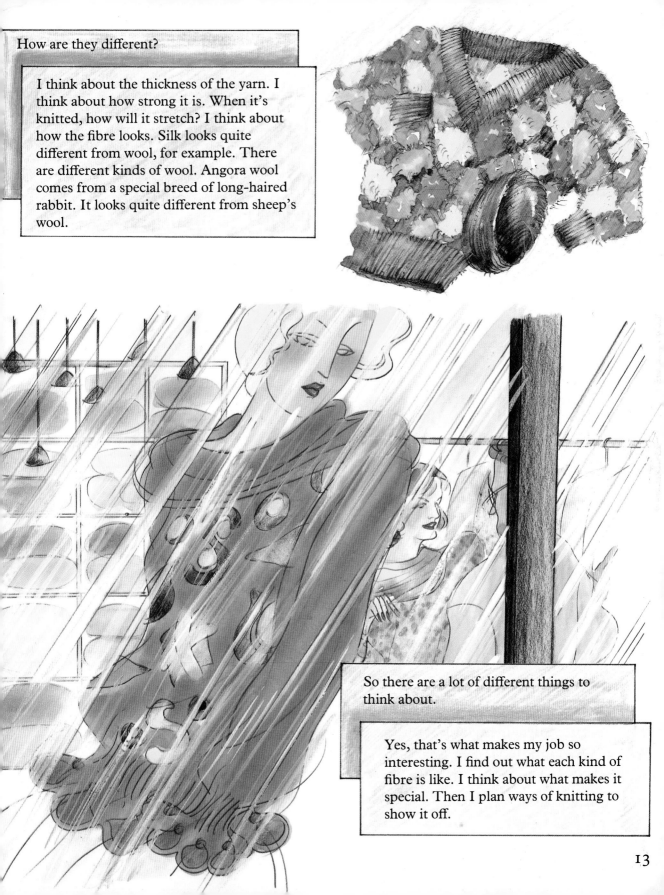

So there are a lot of different things to think about.

Yes, that's what makes my job so interesting. I find out what each kind of fibre is like. I think about what makes it special. Then I plan ways of knitting to show it off.

The Useful Art of Knitting

When Mum sits down to knit at night
Her patterns seem to go just right.
She doesn't even have to look;
She can knit and read a book.
But, oh, the worry
And the flurry
When I sit
And try to knit!
My stitches always get too tight
Or else I drop them out of sight.
I split the wool and big holes come,
I pass my knitting back to Mum.
I grizzle and I grumble,
I struggle and I mumble.
I feel just like that girl Matilda
('The effort very nearly killed her.')
Mum says, 'Don't worry, try once more.'
I throw my knitting on the floor.
We both get cross; I go to bed
And a wonderful dream comes into my head:
When my knitting is finished
I shall win First Prize
for
The Most Original
Best Ventilated
Multi-coloured
Complicated
Scarf
Knitted by a Demented Spider
For an Oddly-shaped Snake
With a Very
Sore Throat.

Katherine Craig

Chester's Undoing

Chester Lester Kirkenby Dale
Caught his sweater on a nail.
As Chester Lester started to travel
So his sweater began to unravel.
A great long trail of crinkly wool
Followed Chester down to school.
Then his ears unravelled!
His neck and his nose!
Chester undid from his head
To his toes.
Chester's undone, one un-purl, two un-plain,
Who's got the pattern to knit him again?

Julie Holder

Weaving and felting

Weaving

Another way of making threads into fabric is by weaving. Weaving uses two threads; the **warp** and the **weft**. A weaver uses a machine called a loom to weave fabric.

Denim is a woven material used to make jeans. It was first made in a town in France called Nîmes. It became know as 'De Nîmes' meaning 'from Nîmes' and is now called denim.

Warp
The long warp threads run along the length of the fabric.

Weft
The weft thread is woven across, in and out between the warps and taken back again in the opposite direction.

Modern loom in Korea

Felting

Fibres can be made into fabrics in a third way, by felting. This is usually done with wool fibres. They are not spun into threads first. The fibres are made hot and wet and then they are pounded and pressed together. This makes a fabric that is both tough and soft at the same time. It is very difficult to tear. Soft toys for babies are often made from felt. Can you think why?

Herringbone

Twill

Tweed

What clothes are you wearing today that are made of woven fabric? Look through a magnifying glass at some woven fabric. Can you see the threads going in different directions? Draw a picture of some woven fabric seen through a magnifying glass.

Different patterns can be made by using different arrangements of the warp and the weft. A fabric called twill is made by weaving between two threads at a time. The pattern twists sideways down the length of the material. Different coloured warps and wefts are used to make checks.

Stretchability

One of the things a designer needs to know about a fabric is its stretchability. Test a variety of fabrics so that you can rate them for their stretchability. Make sure you include some knitted, some woven and some felted fabrics in your test. Record their stretchability on a chart. Give each fabric a score of up to five points for each type of stretchability –
1 means not at all stretchy, 5 means very stretchy. How can you make sure that the test is fair?

Try stretching the fabrics in different ways – up and down, diagonally and across. Which way of pulling stretches the fabric most? Do the three different types of fabric – knitted, woven and felted – stretch the same amount?

What happens to the fabric when you let go? Does it go back to its original shape?

Can you think of three things you can use each of your fabrics for?

Special materials

Sometimes we need absorbent materials, which soak up water, to use as towels, tea-towels or dishcloths. But at other times we use materials to prevent us getting wet.

Many of our clothes are made with materials which are coated with wax or which have chemicals added to them to make them waterproof. Carpets are usually sprayed with a waterproofing chemical too so that spilt drinks can be wiped up easily before they can soak into the carpet.

Other materials have chemicals added to make them fire- or flame-resistant. Nowadays, furniture is often covered with a fireproof material which is treated to stop the furniture catching fire so quickly.

Can you think of a way to test different fabrics to find out which ones are best at keeping water out and which ones let most water through? You can make a chart to record your findings.

Can you invent a way to make fabric waterproof?

Can you think of people who need to wear waterproof or fireproof clothing in their jobs?

Do you have any waterproof clothes? When do you wear them?

Synthetic fibres

Parachute with synthetic cords and ropes

Look at the labels in your clothes. How many different sorts of fibre are you wearing?

For thousands of years, fabrics were made from natural fibres that came from plants and animals. About a hundred years ago, artificial or **synthetic** fibres were invented.

The first synthetic fibre was made from cellulose. This is a substance which is found in wood pulp and cotton. It is dissolved into a thick, gummy liquid and squirted through tiny holes called spinnerets. It dries into thin fibres called rayon which can be spun, woven and dyed like silk. Scientists had wanted to make a synthetic silk because a disease had killed off many silkworms.

Can you think of a fair way to compare the strengths of some natural and some synthetic threads?

Try making a synthetic fibre. Squirt a little milk, gently, into a cup of vinegar. A white fibre will be made; but it has no strength. Synthetic fibres are dried and treated to make them stronger.

Other synthetic fibres such as nylon, polyester and acrylic are made from chemicals. These fabrics are strong and easy to wash and dry. They can be made to feel almost like wool, cotton or silk. Synthetic fibres make tough ropes and string. Synthetic fibres are often stronger than natural fibres as they do not rot like natural fibres and they are not attacked by pests like moths. Synthetic fibres are also usually cheaper to manufacture into fabrics and clothes than natural fibres. They are normally cheaper to produce too. But people like Patricia Roberts prefer natural fibres because they feel more comfortable, they dye better and they can be knitted by hand more easily.

Windsurfing board with synthetic sail

Colours and patterns

We can produce a great variety of fabrics by weaving or knitting the threads to give different textures and patterns. Colour also adds to the pattern and variety of fabrics. Natural dyes are a traditional way of making fabrics in many beautiful colours. People have used fruits, flowers, roots or tree bark to make dyes. Insects, snails and shells have been used too. In Roman times, people learned to make red, blue, purple, yellow, orange, black and brown dyes.

Dyes can be made from onion skins, bilberries, lichens, walnuts, buds, bark and leaves. But nowadays, we mostly use dyes made from chemicals. These dyes can produce hundreds of different shades. Some materials will take dyes very easily when they are boiled together. But usually a **mordant** is needed. A mordant helps the fabric to absorb the dye.

There are many different ways to use dyes. A simple way to make coloured patterns on fabric is to crush or tie the fabric so that the dye does not reach all the material. This leaves patches of undyed colour amongst the dyed areas.

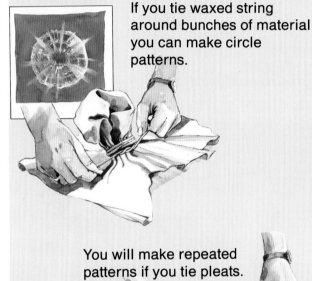

If you tie waxed string around bunches of material you can make circle patterns.

You will make repeated patterns if you tie pleats.

If, with your teacher, you have made some dyes using onion skins, try dyeing some fabric without using a mordant to fix the dye. Now try washing the fabric using a detergent. Does the dye come out? Now try dyeing the same sort of fabric again, but this time use either salt or a commercial mordant to fix the dye. Again, wash the fabric using detergent. How much dye comes out this time?

Shapes or pictures can be drawn on material with hot liquid wax. The wax stops the dye reaching the fabric. We call this 'resisting' the dye. More wax can be added before using another coloured dye. This method is called batik.

You can make good patterns using a stencil. The stencil will help you make the dye go just where you want it.

Try making dyes from other vegetables, fruits or leaves. Test different fabrics to see which ones dye best.

Can you make patterns on the fabrics by tying them in knots before you put the dye on?

23

Glossary

boll
A boll is the seed pod of a cotton plant. It is a ball of cotton fibres with many seeds in it.

to card
When wool or cotton is carded, it is combed so that the fibres are untangled and made to lie in one direction.

cocoon
A silkworm spins a protective silk casing around itself before it turns into a moth. This is its cocoon. Caterpillars of other butterflies and moths also spin cocoons.

fibre
A single strand of something, such as wool, cotton or hair is a fibre.

fleece
The wool from a sheep is called a fleece before it is cleaned and carded.

mordant
A mordant is something which is added to dye to help the dye stick to the fabric. When a mordant has been added, less of the dye runs out in the wash.

synthetic
Synthetic means artificial. In this book it is used to refer to fabrics that have not been directly made from natural threads and fibres.

thread
A thread is a number of fibres twisted or spun together.

warp
The warp is the thread that runs from the top to the bottom of a piece of cloth as it is being woven.

weft
The weft is the thread that runs from side to side as a piece of cloth is being woven.

yarn
Yarn is another word for thread. It is often used in knitting.